Womb

WEAVING OF MY BEING

Ahava Shira

*To Sarta(?),
your beauty helps me
know my own,
aShira*

BUTTERFLY PRESS
Vancouver, Canada

*To David,
for your support and "attention-
water to water, soul to soul. aShira*

Copyright © 1998 by Ahava Shira

All rights reserved. No part of this publication may be reproduced or transmitted in any form or by any means, electronic or mechanical, including photocopying, recording, or any information storage and retrieval system, without permission in writing from the publisher.

Published in 1998 by
Butterfly Press
Suite 267 - 4438 West 10th Avenue
Vancouver, B.C.
V6R 4R8
Tel. (604) 878-9660
Fax (604) 221-8119
E-mail:butterflypress@yahoo.com

Canadian Cataloguing in Publication Data

Shira, Ahava, 1967-
   Womb - Weaving of my being

   Poems .
   ISBN 0-9684619-0-5

I . Title.
PS8587.H566W65 1998   C811` .54   C98-911159-8
PR9199.3.S5148W65 1998

Book design: Longhouse Communications
Photography: Paul Schulz
Editorial direction: Mahaka Shira

Printed on recycled paper using vegetable based inks.
Printed and bound in Canada.

Thank you to: Mom for giving from your heart, Auntie Lily for opening my eyes to art, Rita for the courage to begin, Dad for being there in rhyme and reason, Donna and Monica for your generous presence, Christie and Krista for your intimate friendship, Abby for faith in practice, Tev for your magical inspiration, Phil and Betty, Roy and John for your teachings in the lodge of life, Susanna and Nexus for helping me receive the dream, and everyone else who has guided and supported me throughout this creative process, especially Mahaka and Jerry for believing in my voice.   Blessed Be.

for **MAHAKA**

w o m b

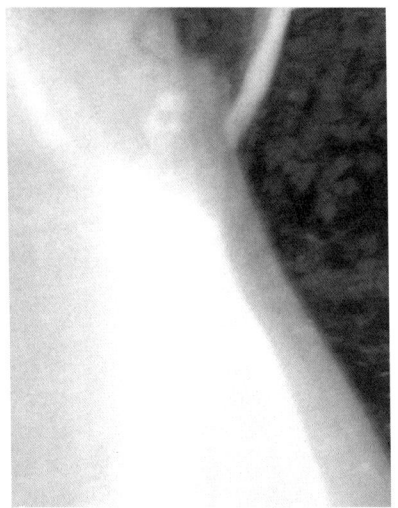

Womb

There is a lesson in the unknowing
a voice full of sound and fury
wisdom resounding, and yet
i doubt i fear i lose my way
in the face of another
i forget the magic of
my own miscommunication
when patiently attended
unfolds for me in meaning
clearer than another's words spoken

Thus i'm drawn to wonder
why is it ever i hesitate
turn myself out
read every line as if it were my body
moving through the rhythms
shake my head
and fail to realize
it is all written inside

There is no message on the floor
no where to look but feel
the fabric of my self
crafted, slowly
in intricate detail
a solitary motif followed throughout

This is my work
i cannot show you what i do
i have to watch and listen
as the patterns are woven out of my being
over time

Contents

- 8. Trees

- 10. Grace
- 11. The Game
- 13. Echo
- 14. Rape Poem
- 17. Magnetic

- 18. Stillness

- 20. Food For Thought
- 21. Coma
- 22. Refusing To Eat
- 24. Prozac
- 26. These Boots
- 27. Mother
- 28. Eagles Soaring
- 29. Shelter in the Wilderness
- 30. Space
- 31. Butterfly

- 32. Emergence

- 34. Grace(reprise)
- 36. Mondschmerzen
- 38. Labyrinths
- 40. Lifeblood
- 42. Intimate
- 43. The Good Wet
- 45. The Secret

- 47. Imperfect

- 50. I Am a Woman
- 54. Bosom Body
- 57. My Body and Me
- 58. Mystical Braided Ancient Mama
- 60. Something Going On
- 61. The Fool
- 62. Ripples

Trees

Trees
tall bare unmoving

People
crying laughing

Me
feeling

GRACE

She used to live
in a hole in the couch
but the noise
from the television
became unbearable
so she moved

to a crack
in the bathroom sink

where
she only had to feel
his slimy hands on her
at rare intervals
between the commercials
there
she could lay back
against the cool porcelain
and let the water spill over her
sanctifying her naked body
with every wash

At night
when he was asleep
she would spread herself out
fully   around the basin

like his body
against the couch

and listen
as the thick drops
filtered out of the faucet
heavy   in anticipation
until they would meet
her skin and theirs
making love

The Game

He lifted me up
i turned around and around
the wind carrying me
from his hands into the air

i let him touch me
let his fingers move
from there to there
it felt good inside my body

A new feeling inside my body
warm and tingly
it was a game i learned to play
first he would touch me
then i would quickly run away

i wanted to feel happy
to let the music move me
as his fingers seduced me
it grew wet between my legs
then i would leave feeling guilty

Little children aren't supposed to be touched
neither there nor there
little children are supposed to be loved like this
open arms   warm hands   big hugs
little children are supposed to smile and be silly
putting their feet inside sweater arms
little children are supposed to laugh and dance

He lifted me up
i wanted to be turned around and around
i wanted to be loved
i didn't want to keep hearing the sound of their
voices screaming

i wanted up
so high i could hear silence

and see mountains
he took me there

Only each time i landed
with a thud
it hurt

Still i let him lift me up
more light please
closer to the sun
the stars

He lifted me up
I don't think we knew what we were doing
he was 12
i was 8

Maybe i was lifting him up
letting him dance
setting him free
to feel the wind against his cheeks

Maybe i was holding his hand

and together we turned
around and around
and
around

Echo

Sometimes his hands are instruments
making music with my body
pulling strings of soft caress
and sweet sensation
evoking melodies
touching sounds buried deep
uncovering fears left silent by time

Sometimes his hands take me dancing
between the folds   two lips tremble
as i sway and shake
pleasing feeling
making me cry out for more
another gentle spin around the floor

Sometimes his hands aren't touching me
and yet their voices echo through me

Rape Poem

The fountain pushes her over
to one side
its milk white spout
curdling around the
stilted ankles
a deafening stench
makeshift fury
marks eons lifetimes
of hellbent scurry
toward forgiveness
forgiveness
for- who is she meant to
give her life -ness
for a meaning
beyond this present pain
a golf club lodged inside
her trapezius swinging
hinged to a past
suckers hang low against
the defense
floor tiles creak
abandon the sun
the stars
the floating spacecraft
strap her wrists closed
to the shuttle
spaceship descending
      descending
going underwater
    underground
    under the
meadow
lies a coffin
black stained oak, cedar
flat bottom

satin sheets
a mattress of creepy crawlers
her decaying skin smelling fresh
as the latrine
being emptied again
her skinless bones
turning over
the words on her tongue
the words on her lips
        on her chest falling
down
face flat against the dirt
he raises her skirt
a deathening chill
rises up
as he thrusts
her white panties
now stained with hatred
and devotion
she chews on the earth
giving her silent words
to the Mother

can you hear me

she chews silent
his angry hand
ripping the dress
scraping the skin
melting the love he is
making her sick with his love
making her sick with this love
making her sick
with his
dick

fucking the shit out of her
as she lies silently
chewing the dirt
her skirt a blanket now
she grabs onto and suckles
his face in front
of her now
he has turned her over
he has turned her over
shutting her life
she has eyes now
to see the pain
of swords it feels like
glue in her cunt
piss in her mouth
shit on her body
the buzz of razors
skinning her flesh
she disintegrates
her eyes fall back against the earth
whispering

I Saw Him Do It
You Won't Believe Me
I Saw Him Do It

he stops and zips up his fly
wipes his hand on her skirt
fumbling for the keys in his shirt pocket
a hand between his hair pushing it
back against the sky
the moon was there
he notices the sliver
then ducks into the car
slams the door

in the glove compartment
are the remnants of lunch
a half eaten
ham and cheese sandwich
on white bread
the plastic comes off easily
and he takes a bite

her eyes are speaking with the earth speaking

I SAW HIM DO IT
THEY WON'T BELIEVE ME
I SAW HIM DO IT

Magnetic

The magnetic impulse
of my hand gliding across the page
the words emerging from a soreness
inside of me
a hollowness that surrounds my heart
like a tree whose trunk is a shelter
for some homeless animal

Stillness

Stillness

    moves me forward   my hands
       touching reaching grasping

                                    Stillness
  pulls me back
  shifting weight
    steady and

                center stage

somewhere
deep within
a loud echo   bellows
her angry mouth waters
saliva drips
d
o
w
n
      u ⁿ d ^u l ^a t ⁱ n ^g   b ^e l ^l _y

breathshort
becoming   l o n   g   e   r

head rests inside the shell
carrying the world
she waits
and watches
slowly her eyes
  open   out
       into the
           darkness

Food For Thought

Thoughts interrupt
standing in a shallow wood
i dig a hole
there is comfort in denying
what is mine
chasing pennies in a well
i swallow hard
more than a handful
        a mouth full
        a belly full of frozen yeses

Put some sugar in my bowl
i taste the freedom with my mind

Too much food
for thoughts have a way
of entering my field of vision
carrying me away

There is no need to feast or famine
i have what i need
right here and now
old habits die hard
so hard
to trust the love of my own breath against the world
so hard
to let the emptiness fill me
so hard
to see the emptiness as full

COMA

Theirs was a marriage of dissension
an accident with irreparable damage
done to the child with the least resistance
full speed
head on
no time to get out of the way
the point of contact:

there was none

I lived in a world where everything was dead
including myself
the trees didn't have life
the people didn't breathe
the earth was something we trampled upon
everything was as it was

No myths nor stories nor legends
no animals to be my friends
no life to share the space
with me
i was all alone
and i was so scared

Refusing To Eat

She doesn't want to live
She didn't tell me that
but i see no reason for
refusing to eat
other than being full enough already
still its been days since she's had a mouthful
so empty is she i can barely see her
buried in a shroud of ivory
on a cloud of self-hate and denial
in a state of imperfection
that she couldn't stay alive to appreciate
as the only perfect state there is

Why doesn't she want to live
has she not seen the flowers blooming all around
this spring
or spent some time alone sitting by the ocean with
a journal and an open heart
or felt a lover's arms reach around to shelter her
like the wings of a mother swan

Maybe not

Maybe she's been reading too many magazines and
trying to look like the skinniest one on the cover
or shopping for all the clothes that advertise to
satisfy the other

Maybe she takes her cues
from others' expectations
giving away her beauty and sensuality
for the price of conformity and cultural normalcy

But now
she's another woman
lost

in the body image war
their ammunition is found
in every corner store
sold over the counter
available to anyone who chooses
to be seduced   innocently
by the promises of Glamour
that have nothing to do with
who we really are
or how we can achieve the attention
we all deserve to feel

She doesn't want to live
her breath grows fainter
and her eyes shut tight

Prozac

Inside uncertain frames
the reference to eating   the stains
devouring leftovers
removing signs of life of soul
extinguishing unnecessary burdens
with a chew and a swallow
mantra of a master of excessive minding

the stove blinks
its coiled eyes turn to the refrigerator
who shivers
"what more can i give you"
the freezer chortles to itself
oblivious to the heated
psychological formula
destitute the sink spills out witticisms
joining the round table with its own noble concerns

around the house
a thick paste of defamation hovers
ceiling high
ransacks spiritual children
visitors of angels
looking for a way in

the door slams
the toilet seat stays up
body recoils   recognizes voices
from the vestibule
delivering sermons
the wallpaper arguing acceptance
while the gagging echoes louder
tiles fume beneath bony knees
seated   defeated
a litany of supporters vie for headspace
in the crowded atmosphere

sooner or later
the couch clears its throat
interrupted by the tea kettle
whispering altruisms

furnished-
the apartment ad said-

When looking for a home
there are many DISadvantages
to being a woman
on PROZAC

These Boots

These boots
weren't made for walking
or running
or catching a runaway bus
on the other side of the avenue
as traffic heads straight for you
and your partner's wearing sensible shoes

These boots weren't made for pleasure
cause they're not fit to measure
and the heel's too high to treasure

These boots weren't made for men
or anyone who wants to wander for hours
through fields of clearcut forest

These boots weren't bought for cheap

These boots
 that i no longer walk in

weren't made for me

Mother

What's in a name ?
i   who leave no traces of
the person i once was
or so i've tried
over and over
changing lives like clothes
the wash cycle of my life never ends

Mother
i wanted so much to not be like you
maybe my words are different
but the meanings they evoke remain the same

A clean slate is never easy to obtain
so we keep at it
over and over
each of us in our own compulsive way
scrubbing away at the surface grime
yet too afraid to go deeper
to look at what's underneath
our need for neatness
no mess
keep it tidy so nobody will suspect
What a meticulous home !

i can't seem to get mine to shine like hers
the blood stains
and the wounds don't have a chance to heal

We try Mom we try
to no avail
failing
now i must admit my defeat
accept my losses
and ask for help

Why couldn't you ever ask for help
and not from me ?

Help me Shechina
the spirit that dwells within...

Eagles Soaring

How do i close the door
and open up the sky
to eagles soaring
reaching into my soul to weave
the dreams into my being
flesh and bloody
a wounded willow tree
bending down to receive the call of truth
crouching behind fears and long-past ways ?

Shelter In The Wilderness

some calm amidst the storm
rest my tired body
bruised from the strain of too much remembering
and torn open by the agony of the unknown

what comes next
a woman a jew a conscious self
i know no way to choose what's best

Let me live inside awhile
where the darkness
holds the key
the doorway to my soul has been locked
it has been kept locked, barred, bolted
back up against the metal wall   back and forth
the movement jars

who am i ?
what lies hiding waiting to emerge?
are these my questions?
can i stand differently, see differently
hear the voice that speaks to me of answers?

Fanny finds a way to let me know i am not alone
She holds me with her invisible arms
and speaks to me of a love
that is unconditional and whole

A woman's tale is woven through the threads of my
imagination
it is all i have to show
it whispers:
keep LOVE alive
      keep LOVE alive
            keep LOVE alive

Space

One arm twisted behind my back
stopping the flow
crooked neck
straining to feel the ease
of silence
upon its tired bones

i've been holding on for so long
running wild being busy
the silence stops me
and i feel the pain of surrender

just beyond this wall of fear i feel
there is a pool of light and love and freedom
i take a step
then wait and watch and listen

i am as the plants and trees
i breathe and sway and live from day to day
i dream and die and count the ways
i have been blessed with life

and now another and another
felt nagging at my sleeves
suckling my heavy bosom
laden with fear and hope

they are my buried children
come to love me awake
if i let them
open up my heart   my soul my being
creating space
for the little ones to breathe on their own

Butterfly

These days
it's like the world falling down
at my feet
i want to pick it up
let it nuzzle at my breast
warm its fragile hands
that have been too busy doing the devil's work

But the only baby i find at my bosom
is the one gnawing at me
from the other side

inside

and this one's
growing up too fast
she wants to fly before
she can crawl
so i try to rock her back to sleep

But nothing is gonna stop her from
putting her two little feet on the ground
and walking straight out of my arms
into the Light

Emergence

Soft and shiny
her tiny head pokes through the crevice
shivering with new life

A sound hollow and unsettling
like a bear cub caught in a human trap
forcing its way through
struggling with dignity

She inches her way out of the hole
self-forming
   evolving
      emerging

Grace (reprise)

She used to live
in a hole in the couch
but that day the elevator opened
and the kid came home to stay
was more than she could take
even the crack in the sink
wasn't far enough away
for her

the noise grew louder
the touch grew more violent
and the tears
from the sympathetic faucet
couldn't cover all the wounds
she fell back asleep
safe within a dream
but no sooner than her body
resting softly in the waters
did his hands come down upon her

She ran away the next day
left all her stuff
but got herself away in time
to find her heart still beating
like a caged elephant
never forgetting what was really going on
down the drain   her life
the day after day of pain

She found her way back to loving
and it wasn't just another basin
a different type of cage
the rage caught up to her
she held it in her gut
looked her feelings in the face

and with Grace
she became
more than a pronoun
a living breathing name

running free   the earth
she set it free   the trees
she set it free
the guilt   the shame   the doubt
she set them down and she was free

No more a silent woman
keeping her body tucked away
inside the sink

she went another way
her way
home

it all started with a crack
and some tears
and the drops
how they made love

Now she knows
she can never stay
in the same place too long   before
someone other
wants to sit in on her self
having fun   and so

She keeps on moving…

Mondschmerzen*

throughout the night and
into the morning
filling my dreams with my body and
my body with pain
i feel Her aliveness inside me
preparing me for the journey
claiming Her time to release
The Woman of the Moon
weaving a path through my womb
trailing red stains
marking death
seeking life
rendering me barren but
open

She passes through my labyrinth
She has been this way before
Her slippery shape
moist with the fire
of my soul   expressing
Her thick breath
dampening the flames
as She descends

soaking up the dew
in my layers of softness
then feeding Herself
with this source of liquid abandon
She flows toward freedom
extending beyond the boundaries
of my hollow
She explodes
passionately
drenching me with scarlet rain

my skin responding with excitement
absorbing the sensations of Her omnipresence
within and without

36.

    i stand naked before Her
         and i know
      i am beautiful
        and round like Her
for we were created in Her image

i behold Her in the sky
and remember
that
by the cycle
of my womb
She speaks to me
and
i listen

* moon pains

Labyrinths

Milky white
the waters pour out of me
tracing a cycle
of birth
and death
a story of internal expression
written in my body's way
a land   hostile from the battles
waged against its crimson suit
once armoured and dangerous
explosive to the mind

But labyrinths love seasons
of growth and decay
expectations filtering out
in the shifting
day to day
then   flowers bloom
and castles of clouds
form communities
the sky opens
shaking free a lunar reign
full of that liquid love
our babies cry for

and now the swords are sinking
beneath the tender surface
exposing a millenia of empty executions
and for once the blood is left to
run   and
         drip   and
                  flow
spreading out over vast deserted landscapes

staining the barren space with
pomegranate dew
painting it red and hot
like the inside of a woman's body
in that time of hers
when she has access to   all worlds
all wisdom

LIFEBLOOD

It feels good to be in the shelter
of my moontime
my time
to be inside myself
to feel the rhythm of my body in motion
the flow of life
so close to home and heart

lifeblood stirring
down and out it goes
taking parts of me with it
i no longer need
shedding skin
another layer peeling off
revealing new life not yet born
a vulnerable child

with open eyes and tender heart
still beating from within
gentle spirit soothing
as its thin skin becomes sensitive
to touch from other
a self created by mother
giving birth to freedom

circle of women surrounding me
holding my body
as i descend
deep down into the earth to bear
my wounded lover
another side of me awakening
together we lay buried
limb against limb
nuzzling each other in the darkness
where no one can see us
alone we revel in this blood mystery

And then

feeling their hands on me
i ascend the cool paradise
back up toward the circle
i surface

red and full of fury
eager to tell her story
to the listener or the reader or the seer

i loosen up my naked flesh
look up toward the brightest star
and smile, laugh loud

Sweet Wisdom watches
from behind Her sacred willow tree
grinning as She witnesses
a woman full of rhythm in a world that's out of tune

Dripping over my legs and feet
a crimson rain of pearls, rose petals
dancing as they tumble
the scent of love's embracing every curve
my form a fragrant flower
flow er   opening up   and   out

Shine on sisters
sweating   moaning   bursting through the landscape
grounding all our furies
into stories passion plays
that take a year and a day
to pass on   action from the
moving from within
drawing down
  digging in
    rising up
      reaching out

        Starting over....

Intimate

I want to be intimate with myself
i desire to taste my mossy pond   to smell
the dampness of its mist upon my lips
tu lips that enfold and unfold
like a wild lotus my wisdom flower abloom
moist and scented with the aroma of woman

I want to be intimate with myself
i desire to spy my shy bermuda   to know
its textures and colours   the warp and weft
of time against its tender shape
my island passages
coming and going   and coming again

I want to be intimate with myself
i desire to touch my sacred space   to feel
my fingers exploring its hallways and secret rooms
as my spirit comes alive in every nook and cranny
and i linger long moments   listening
at my altar of altars my place of worship

Here is my connection to everything

The Good Wet

I stare at my reflection
my ass pale a pimple on my left cheek
or is it right
from this angle i can't tell

my arms against the carpet
my body propped up
i am sweating from the heat
it is 30 degrees out
and i am excited in this moment
that's what it's all about
this moment and

the taste of cum
the smell of arousal
my flower spread open
like in the middle of a garden
my lily so exuberant to be
paid attention to
to be touched so deeply

My face is shiny a cramp in my right leg
or is it left
i look from between my legs into the mirror
i can't tell

i can't tell
it is forbidden
this bonaqua:
the good wet feeling of
my flesh disappearing into desire

Where am i
who is this sex-crazed woman
that erupts from time to time
she has no inhibitions
shoves things up her cunt
screams at someone " fuck me fuck me "

who do i become
when i am full of self affection
like a mother seducing her kittens
with her milk
i am playing with myself

i am playing with myself
until this scene comes to completion
and i awake to catch myself on all fours
naked from the waist down
slowly i make myself more presentable to the mirror
put my tools away
and smile

Who is this woman
loves to fuck herself
get hot and heavy with her fingers in the mirror

i'd like to get to know her better ...

THE SECRET

The sea licking my knees
skimming the backs of my thighs
i hike my black velour dress up
to give Her more
to let Her in
She doesn't have to knock
knows She is welcome

cool resonance
of salt on skin

i remember this feeling
alone undetermined to move
waiting for rush heat
soft crimson folding
into heart
he knew the way
as She does now

i am still dressed and open
longing for innocent uncrumpled seduction
burying reason
to blush and burn
to secede experience
victory standing still

now She courts my sweetness
cultivates delirium
addresses all my wants by touch
dividing me into Love
and loved

he should have trembled
as i did   when alone
how did we hide so much excitement
strap lust onto two adolescent bodies
and float deep into unseen
places on the couch

Now She leads me back
into unseen
floating deep my body's
lust for hidden excitement
travels narrow canals
toward release
my secret

i never thought i'd find another
so willing

but it is Her vastness
that soothes guilt
for erotic sensuality

She responds to my presence
no questions no conditions
She accepts non-conformity
revels in the incanting allure
of my flesh around her ocean
comes into me to feed Herself

remember
comes into me to feed Herself

the flesh of flesh
transcending
ocean from ocean

fixing our eyes on all parts of the sky
She points to the moon
i scream

i'm cuming
i'm cuming
the secret's out
i'm not alone

Imperfect

These words
they come from deep within
from a need to tell the truth
to speak the forbidden
to find the bareness
of this body hidden
under conditioning
she is too beautiful for masks
i am too beautiful for games
to shade my open heart
the raging sorrow is
what's real in me
to set that free
i must believe it is okay to be
like this
imperfect
with sagging tits
a crooked back and panic attacks
fears and pains

i chose a different name
let my hair fall a different way
but still felt the same
shame for not being perfect
i tried to claim the fame of one
who'd figured out
the way to fit in and look thin
but hey you can't see my cellulite beneath my tights

and you can't tell whether i've been abused
but i can feel the abuse i've put myself through
for not being perfect

These words
they come from deep within
from a woman who grew sick from
having to suck my belly in
wearing boots uncomfortable to walk in
caring more about how i looked
than what i felt within
they reveal the hidden
and   free me

        to be

  all

      i am

I Am a Woman

I am a woman am a song am a voice
from Her bosom shouting
crying for attention
for this body
bruised and broken
to be mended

I am a hunter of the life force
within my bones
rattling against their stiff iron frame
a spiritual warrior   bone and marrow mourner
applying the medicine of the Moon
to the battlewounds in me

I am a soul sister survivor
spinning reason into rhythm
and sweeping shoulders
shedding the weight of burdens
long held head high   my spine
becoming aligned to a more
primal motivation
i am shaking the foundations
finding a source of knowledge
that is stronger
than my weakened knees
bending the state of the world
toward the Earth
on Her we depend

Let us lose our sense of suffocation
Breathe Her into you

Now i am full and swollen like Her
with the seeds of creation
swimming inside me
flowing in my valley of lovely forest
watering the earth with my lifestreams
my river of fertility

spreading out in all directions from my
paradise where flesh and blood
are free to mix and mingle
in my garden of fluid delights

I am a fountain in the garden
of my body and soul
a woman who flows
and feels the milky white juices oozing
down between my legs
i press my fingers against my mouth
from down below
tasting and smelling the sweetness
of my nectar against my lips my nose
i am a soft red rose who knows
the beauty of my textures
flavours

Savouring the scent
i close my eyes
and lay me down beneath
Her sacred willow tree
feeling stronger
as i start to tingle

ssshe climbs onto me
from behind
sssliding her sssmooth tongue
over my ssstem
and toward my petals
the ground is cool my roots are hot
my thorns dethroned
sssliding her sequins all over me
sssuddenly

ssshe is inside me
sssustaining this sssatisfying interaction

i feel her rippling through me
my figure surrendering
i am contacting
and receiving a new expression
of being woman
experiencing
voices coming from the depths
of these intimate spaces
my body's sexy places

UTERUS
you tear us leave us be inside of you
i am a stirring shelter nurturing
your creative pleasure

CLITORIS
climb to the peak of my rhapsody in C
save me from the surgeries
i am meant to deliver sensations
from your horns of plenty
to arouse your imaginations
believe in the power of touch

VULVA
vuelva mi amiga sumptuosa bella senora
dame una flora que tu inspira a mi forma
my mouth waters opening through layers
a tenderness that protects our secrets
in another language for you to uncover

CUNT
i am a sprawling meadow with wildflowers
and a trickling brook   but i must warn you to
honour my luscious countrysides
for i only offer my wellspring to those who
respect my right to love and NO

VAGINA
my shapely vessel expands to welcome your
generous donations   i love attention
see my muscles smile in gratitude
for the gift from you to me
when life begins to move beyond the waiting
i am there to care for its safe passage

WOMB
i am a warm retreat   oceanic entreat
come   and rest your will to be
heart beating
embrace the time alone within the comfort
of your moon cabin

I am a woman who stays close to home
sowing seeds in solitude
where alone i reap the bounty
gathering all i need around me
i am a tree of life overflowing
with the fruits of my labours
a living body that breathes and empties
consuming my desire to be other than
who i am already

I   AM   A   WOMAN

Bosom Body

Sinking back inside my sacred skin
the din is breaking
my body aching for the mystery
the unknown song that sings beneath its pains
a wild refrain softly dances from my lips
seducing me to join the boogie
down to the underworld
nocturnal wonderworlds
awaiting me

one more time i'm on this ouroboros
spinning circle
medicine wave
the cycle carries me when i am present to it
it stirs my imagination
heightens my creative excitation
it makes an honest woman out of me
unleashes the spirit of the Goddess in me
i am released into the abundant atmosphere
of rivers rolling
i am glad to be here

"Pamper me"
there, they had their way
"Don't move too fast,
don't go too far away
i need your attention
and physical affection,

leave me a space
throughout the day
in as many ways as you can
love me nurture me
let your tears water my landscape
your flowers need showers today"

Pencil in hand
my left side has its plans

the right's doing fine
the left deserves rhyming pleasures
scented endeavours
aromatherapy sure fits in nice
to my scheme of things
the dream of being inside my body
i'm coming closer

My breasts need their say
they've rarely made their way into my words
i love them a lot
but what's this i've not really given them
a chance to share

Take it away, bosom buddies... !

"Who are we what are we about
if there's loving you want then why
haven't you figured it out
we are right here in front of you
at the heart of the matter
Mater
Mother
we are the key to your self-mothering abilities

We want your affection, love and attention
we want it here and we want it now
we are so beautiful
but you are so dutiful
Hey lady, love your breasts!

We are not guests in your house
whom you choose to receive every once in a while
we live here and always have
we have the right to say yes or goodnight
to keep others away from your land
you have been a fool for love
giving us away to the highest bidder

Quit it
take your space when you need it
when there's trouble
just leave it all behind
it'll work itself out in time
meanwhile you'll feel sublime and respected

Truth is
there is no more time for childish conflict
give it up and use your silence
now's your chance to be mindful of me
your bosom body

I want you to stop running around
there's nowhere to go
give it up or you are bound to suffer
Get quiet
watch out for your diet
you know what's good for you
and what's not

Work hard doing the things that you like
and you will start to feel alright

And don't ever doubt that you deserve
all the beauty you've unearthed
it's not outside of you
The Navajo teach the Beauty Way
it is how we are to live this moment
each day

Play, have fun, be juicy
and full of creativity
to help yourself see the beauty
Yours is needed by all of us

Share yourself truly"

My Body and Me

Dancing
where there is nobody but me
to laugh and applaud wildly
encore i say to myself
more time to dance for me

i thought i had to dance for them
to prove i am somebody
to strut my stuff and be good
i thought i had to be try to be good
i thought i had to be really good

i left that world
when i found out
that being good
isn't what it's really all about
i opened a space inside my chest
built a nest inside
just for the two of us
my body and me

i live there now
i'm never going back
those advertisements
turn my heart to lack
i've gone away
i've found a home
there are more who will come soon

Self-protection ?
it's called wholeness and self-love
authentic preservation of my integrity
they tried to rip the life from out of me

now they can't find me

Mystical Braided Ancient Mama

I look away
not used to seeing myself so clearly
this innocence is new to me
and i want to let it stay
wrap me in its limbs
i billow
the wind blows through me
a gratitude surrounds me
it doesn't matter who i am
or may pretend to be
the wind blows through me
and the love unveils me

Kiss me life
make me your lover
underneath the cover of your crimson sheath
the sun is setting on another way of being
how easy now to find the rhapsody
amid the rugged wilderness
my emotional range of old growth
i will never cut me down again
though i may sway and bend

This willow's got a will o' Goddess
living within her forest
This willow's got a will o' lovingkindness
dwelling in her tender roots
This willow's got a will o' passion
flowing through her branches
it looks like laughter, smells like heart
and tastes like "open up, i'm coming out"

I look away
this time to see who is beside me
so glad to feel your arms
go round my trunk
to hug me

This willow's got a will of a child
newly born
and i'm receiving all the love
i never could let inside me
it feels like wildfire
warm against my breast

let the wind blow through me
so that i may blaze unruly
my spine crackling with the heat of Shechina

Mystical Braided Ancient Mama
under your wings i am reddening like blood
roses shadow
my trunk solid

Mystical Braided Ancient Mama
through thorns i have grown into woman
fresh as the day my womb first shared its manna
now my life is held out to nourish you
through them that i touch

the manna of Mama
i come to share with my sisters
the Great Mother's food i feed thee
Here, take and be happy

eat eat my sisters
ess ess meinen schwesters!!

SOMETHING GOING ON

Tell me a story
what's happening inside you
really deep inside   i know there's
something going on
i want to know more

Tell me your story
there are secrets that need revealing i want
to hear you see you feel you
i am listening closely   there is
something going on
i want to know more

Tell me Her story
we've got wisdom a language we've been keeping
inside i want
to free our screaming pleasure to laugh like
children we belong
with tears and joy our hearts surrendering
to the body knowledge we're uncovering

Let's tell each other
because we need to know the language
of the Mother   there is
something that's been
going on in Her e
i want to know more

The Fool

I dance the dance of a fool
that becomes what it becomes
without a thought of what it could have been
i am the fool dancing
my body the present
unfolding before my eyes
a moving picture of a paradise
my body the paint
as i explore my many colours on canvas
i breathe and the image changes
each moment a new shape emerging from the stone
as i mold myself around the emptiness
the fool's paradise
i lift and bend and curl and lunge and reach
beyond my knowing
as the shadows play upon my skin
absorbing the shattered glass
the mirror is gone
and i remain standing here
without a taste of my own mind
i am still and free from time and memory

I am a dancing fool
living on the edge of my own two feet
i trust that they will lead and i will follow

Ripples

There is no end
to what can be said
with words
they are like a shelter now
that i have come to sit beneath
keeping me warm and safe
pleasant company
i am never alone
with so many words
still to be written

every image i reveal is a healing
breathing meaning
into my being

silent notation
steady revelation
ecstatic word association

i climb the page toward its conclusion
i've heard it all once called illusion
but these words
  this pen   my hands
are real to me
and all this imaginary writing
sets my spirit free
so i care not what is said of me
i rest beneath my letter tree
and watch them as they fall
into my poems
like stones that ripple
on the water

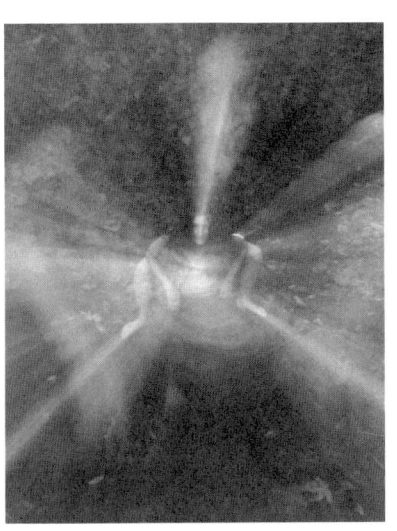